rockschool®

Bass Grade 3

*Performance pieces, technical exercises and in-depth guidance
for Rockschool examinations*

Evergreen House, 2–4 King Street, Twickenham, Middlesex TW1 3RZ
www.rockschool.co.uk

Acknowledgements

Published by Rockschool Ltd. © 2012
Catalogue Number RSK051213
ISBN: 978-1-908920-12-6
Revision 2 | 22 October 2014 | Errata details can be found at *www.rockschool.co.uk*

AUDIO
Recorded at Fisher Lane Studios
Produced and engineered by Nick Davis
Assistant engineer and Pro Tools operator Mark Binge
Mixed and mastered at Langlei Studios
Mixing and additional editing by Duncan Jordan
Supporting Tests recorded by Duncan Jordan and Kit Morgan
Mastered by Duncan Jordan
Executive producers: James Uings, Jeremy Ward and Noam Lederman

MUSICIANS
James Arben, Joe Bennett, Jason Bowld, Larry Carlton, Stuart Clayton, Andy Crompton, Neel Dhorajiwala, Fergus Gerrand,
Charlie Griffiths, Felipe Karam, Kishon Khan, Noam Lederman, DJ Harry Love, Dave Marks, Kit Morgan, Jon Musgrave,
Jake Painter, Richard Pardy, Ross Stanley, Stuart Ryan, Carl Sterling, Henry Thomas, Camilo Tirado, Simon Troup,
James Uings, Steve Walker, Chris Webster, Norton York, Nir Z

PUBLISHING
Fact Files written by Stuart Clayton
Walkthroughs written by Stuart Clayton
Music engraving and book layout by Simon Troup and Jennie Troup of Digital Music Art
Proof and copy editing by Stuart Clayton, Claire Davies, Stephen Lawson, Simon Pitt and James Uings
Publishing administration by Caroline Uings
Cover design by Philip Millard

SYLLABUS
Syllabus director: Jeremy Ward
Instrumental specialists: Stuart Clayton, Noam Lederman and James Uings
Special thanks to: Brad Fuller and Georg Voros

SPONSORSHIP
Noam Lederman plays Mapex Drums, PAISTE cymbals and uses Vic Firth Sticks
Rockschool would like to thank the following companies for donating instruments used in the cover artwork

PRINTING
Printed and bound in the United Kingdom by Caligraving Ltd
CDs manufactured in the European Union by Software Logistics

DISTRIBUTION
Exclusive Distributors: Music Sales Ltd

CONTACTING ROCKSCHOOL
www.rockschool.co.uk
Telephone: +44 (0)845 460 4747
Fax: +44 (0)845 460 1960

Table of Contents

Introductions & Information

Rockschool Grade Pieces

Technical Exercises

Supporting Tests

Additional Information

Welcome to Rockschool Bass Grade 3

Welcome to Bass Grade 3

Welcome to the Rockschool Bass Grade 3 pack. This book and CD contain everything you need to play bass at this grade. In this book you will find the exam scores in both standard bass notation and TAB. The CD has full stereo mixes of each tune, backing tracks to play along to for practice, and spoken two bar count-ins to both the full mixes and the backing track versions of each of the songs.

Bass Exams

For each grade you have the option of taking one of two different types of examination:

- **Grade Exam:** a Grade Exam is a mixture of music performances, technical work and tests. You prepare three pieces (two of which may be Free Choice Pieces) and the contents of the Technical Exercise section. This accounts for 75% of the exam marks. The other 25% consists of: *either* a Sight Reading *or* an Improvisation & Interpretation test (10%), a pair of instrument specific Ear Tests (10%), and finally you will be asked five General Musicianship Questions (5%). The pass mark is 60%.

- **Performance Certificate:** in a Performance Certificate you play five pieces. Up to three of these can be Free Choice Pieces. Each song is marked out of 20 and the pass mark is 60%.

Book Contents

The book is divided into a number of sections:

- **Exam Pieces:** in this book you will find six specially commissioned pieces of Grade 3 standard. Each of these is preceded by a *Fact File*, and each single Fact File contains a summary of the song, its style, tempo, key and technical features, along with a list of the musicians who played on it. Also included is more in-depth information on the genre it is styled upon and relevant techniques you will encounter, as well as recommended further listening. The song itself is printed on two pages and immediately after each song is a *Walkthrough*. This covers the whole song from a performance perspective, focusing on the technical issues you will encounter along the way. Each Walkthrough features two graphical musical 'highlights' showing particular parts of the song. Each song comes with a full mix version and a backing track. Both versions have spoken count-ins at the beginning. Please note that any solos played on the full mix versions are indicative only.

- **Technical Exercises:** you should prepare the exercises set in this grade as indicated. There is also a Fill test that should be practised and played to the backing track.

- **Supporting Tests and General Musicianship Questions:** in Bass Grade 3 there are three supporting tests. You can choose *either* a Sight Reading test *or* an Improvisation & Interpretation test (please choose only one of those), which is then followed by the two mandatory Ear Tests and a set of General Musicianship Questions (GMQs). Examples of the types of tests likely to appear in the exam are printed in this book, while additional examples of both types of tests and the GMQs can be found in the Rockschool *Bass Companion Guide*.

- **Grade 4 Preview:** in this book we have included one of the songs featured in the Grade 4 Bass book as a taster. The piece is printed with its accompanying Fact File and Walkthrough, and the full mix and backing tracks are on the CD.

- **General Information:** finally, you will find the information you need on exam procedures, including online examination entry, marking schemes and what to do when arriving (and waiting) for your exam.

We hope you enjoy using this book. You will find a *Syllabus Guide* for Bass and other exam information on our website: *www.rockschool.co.uk*. Rockschool Graded Music Exams are accredited in England, Wales and Northern Ireland by Ofqual, the DfE and CCEA and by SQA Accreditation in Scotland.

SONG TITLE: OVERRATED
GENRE: ALTERNATIVE ROCK
TEMPO: 125 BPM
KEY: E MINOR

TECH FEATURES: EIGHTH-NOTE LINES
ACCENTS
SLIDES

COMPOSERS: BOB GRACEFUL
& KUNG FU DRUMMER

PERSONNEL: STUART RYAN (GTR)
HENRY THOMAS (BASS)
NOAM LEDERMAN (DRUMS)

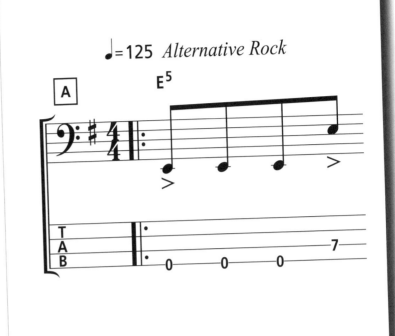

OVERVIEW

'Overrated' is an alternative rock track written in the style of groups such as Foo Fighters, Biffy Clyro and Twin Atlantic. The bassline heard on this track features many hallmarks of alt rock, including pounding root-based lines, offbeat accents and arpeggiated figures. There is also plenty of room for dynamics, thanks to the slides and accents which form parts of the song's bassline.

STYLE FOCUS

Alternative rock is a broad style that draws on many sub-genres. It is common for the alt rock bass player to have a wide-ranging role that encompasses supportive, root-based lines, unison riffs; and in the case of bands like Muse, extended range instruments (five-string bass guitars, for example) and effects pedals. While alt rock basslines can be simple, there is scope for more complex parts too.

THE BIGGER PICTURE

Ex-Nirvana drummer and Foo Fighters frontman Dave Grohl has been central to the development of this branch of alt rock. While playing drums with Nirvana, Grohl began working on demo tapes that formed the basis of the Foo Fighters' first album. Their early records retained the quiet-loud dynamic of Nirvana's music while revealing Grohl's melodic songwriting.

The influence of Foo Fighters is most obvious in two contemporary alt rock groups, both of whom happen to come from the West of Scotland: Biffy Clyro and Twin Atlantic.

Several modern rock bassists have come to the fore in recent years, including the Foo Fighters' Nate Mendel, Chris Wolstenholme of British power trio Muse, Tool's Justin Chancellor and James Johnston of Biffy Clyro. Each of these bass players is a master of different aspects of playing.

RECOMMENDED LISTENING

Foo Fighters have amassed dozens of songs since 1995, the best of which can be found on their *Greatest Hits* (2009). Biffy Clyro's last album *Only Revolutions* (2009) was their commercial breakthrough, but their previous record *Puzzle* (2007) bears a more obvious Foos influence. The latest album by Twin Atlantic *Free* (2011) was the subject of much critical acclaim and is a testament to Grohl and co's enduring legacy.

Overrated

Bob Graceful & Kung Fu Drummer

† Repick slide destination note

Guitar Solo (8 bars)

Walkthrough

A Section (Bars 1–5)
The track opens with an eighth-note based groove with accented octave notes.

Bars 1–3 | *Accented octaves*
The opening bassline is a simple root-based eighth-note line with octaves used to highlight the guitar accents. As you play through each bar, try to keep the eighth-note pulse in your head ("1 & 2 & 3 & 4 &"). The first octave note is played on the 'and' of beat 2, and the second is played on beat 4 (Fig. 1). Remember that these need to be accented, so play them slightly harder.

Bar 4 | *Eighth notes*
This bar is a turnaround figure that leads back to the beginning of the section. Although it contains many rests, this bar is simpler than it looks. The first two notes (B notes) are played on the first beat. Remember to make these the same length. The next note (A) is played on the upbeat, or '&' of beat two, and the final two on beats three and four. Since these are written as eighth notes followed by eighth-note rests, make sure they sound for the correct length.

B Section (Bars 6–10)
The next section of the song features a slightly different line and additional chord changes.

Bars 6–8 | *Tied notes*
A tie is used to connect two notes in this bar. When a tie is used only the first note is sounded and lasts for the duration of both notes. After playing the low E on beat one, the next E falls on the '&' of beat two and is tied into beat three. Nothing is actually played on beat three because the E should still be ringing. The next note is played on the '&' of beat three, followed by two further eighth notes.

C Section (Bars 11–22)
This section contains some arpeggiated chord figures and more eighth-note grooves.

Bars 11–13 | *Arpeggiated powerchords*
These bars feature arpeggiated powerchords. Powerchords consist of a root, fifth and octave. To arpeggiate them simply means to play them one note at a time. Be sure to let the top note of each arpeggio ring into the third beat. The final note in each bar is marked staccato, so play it short and detached.

D Section (Bars 23–30)
This section starts with a series of two-note figures that make use of slides. You have the opportunity here to come up with your own part to play underneath the guitar solo.

Bars 23–26 | *Slides*
Slides are played simply by sliding your fretting finger from one note to the next. For the slide in bar 23, fret the E with your first finger, play it, then slide downwards to the B at the 2nd fret. You should arrive at the B in time to play it on the '&' of beat two (Fig. 2).

Bars 27–30 | *Improvising a bassline*
During this section you are free to play your own line. You should bear in mind that a guitar solo is being played and that your job as the bass player is to lay down a supportive line. You could re-use ideas (but not the actual parts) featured earlier in the song, such as eighth note-based lines or arpeggiated powerchords. Once you have a basic idea to work with, you can then embellish it and make it your own.

E Section (Bars 31–43)
The final section of the song consists mostly of eighth-note lines with slides added.

Bars 31–38 | *Repeating an octave higher*
The first four bars of this section have a simple eighth-note line based on the root of each chord. When this line repeats in bars 35–38, it is played an octave higher. This adds variety and excitement as the song builds to a climax.

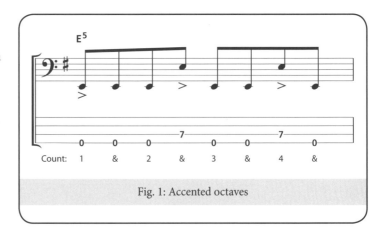

Fig. 1: Accented octaves

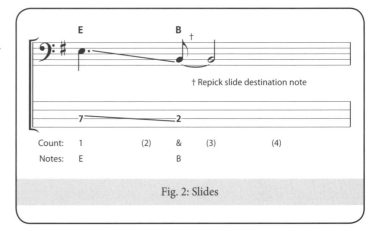

Fig. 2: Slides

Old Bones Blues

SONG TITLE: OLD BONES BLUES
GENRE: BLUES
TEMPO: 115 BPM
KEY: E MINOR

TECH FEATURES: SWUNG EIGHTH NOTES
WALKING BASSLINES
IMPROVISATION

COMPOSER: KIT MORGAN

PERSONNEL: KIT MORGAN (GTR)
HENRY THOMAS (BASS)
NOAM LEDERMAN (DRUMS)
PETE COGGINS (HARP)

OVERVIEW

'Old Bones Blues' is a blues piece written in the style of guitarists like Gary Moore, Eric Clapton and Jeff Beck. The bass guitar plays a supportive yet active role, usually with walking basslines that outline the chord progression. Mastering this is essential because the bass needs to outline the harmony clearly while the guitarist is soloing.

STYLE FOCUS

Blues songs are often based on the 12-bar blues format and 'Old Bone Blues' is no exception to the rule. This song has a swung eighth-note feel, which is also common to the genre. Blues bassists commonly play walking basslines that are based heavily on chord tones, with chromatic passing notes used to connect the different chords. While there are many common walking bass figures, most blues bass guitarists would improvise their lines.

THE BIGGER PICTURE

Blues is a wide ranging genre with many different forms, from acoustic to electric and slide. Acoustic blues developed in the Mississippi delta and was pioneered by artists like the legendary Robert Johnson, whose virtuosity secured his place in blues history. By contrast, the electric sound of Chicago blues players such as Muddy Waters shaped a harder sound based around a full band.

Through the British Blues Boom of the 1960s and guitarists like Eric Clapton, blues entered the mainstream and grew in popularity. In the 1970s and 1980s, Texan blues guitar legend Stevie Ray Vaughan also brought the style to a new audience. Today, blues is thriving through blues rock artists like Joe Bonamassa and singer-songwriter John Mayer.

Blues has produced many superb bassists too: most notably Jack Bruce (Cream), Donald 'Duck' Dunn (The Blues Brothers Band/Booker T. & the M.G.'s) and Tommy Shannon (Stevie Ray Vaughan).

RECOMMENDED LISTENING

To get to grips with blues, listen to 'Walking By Myself', 'Still Got the Blues', and 'Stormy Monday' by Gary Moore, plus 'Born Under A Bad Sign' and 'Crossroads' by Cream. Jeff Beck's 'Beck's Bolero' should be on your playlist, along with 'Sweet Home Chicago' by The Blues Brothers Band and 'Oh Well' by the first (bluesy) incarnation of Fleetwood Mac.

Old Bones Blues

Kit Morgan

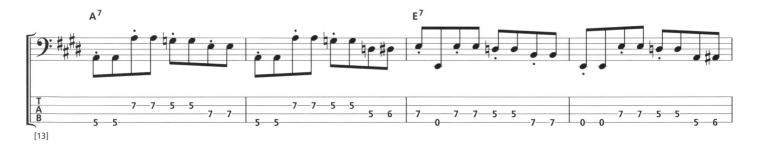

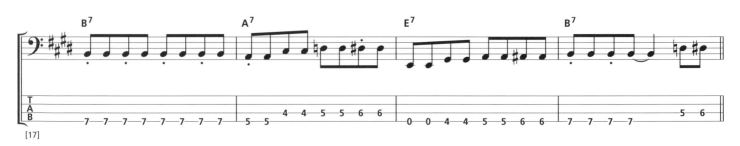

Guitar Solo (8 bars)

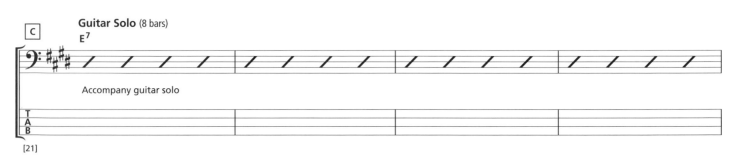

Accompany guitar solo

This music is copyright. Photocopying is illegal.

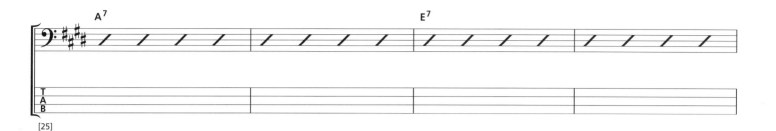

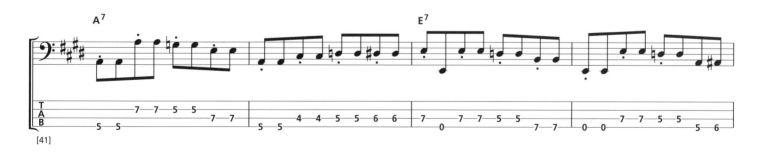

Bass Grade 3

Walkthrough

A Section (Bars 1–4)

The intro to 'Old Bones Blues' is a four-bar blues turnaround figure that is the same as the last four bars of the 16-bar format used throughout the song.

Bars 1–49 | *Swing feel*

The swing feel used throughout the song must be established by the bass from the start. As the tempo indication shows, the pair of eighth notes should be played as long-short.

Bars 2–3 | *Walking basslines*

There are two classic walking bass figures used in these bars (Fig. 1). In bar 2, the bass starts on the root of the A^7 chord, moves up to the major third (C♯), then walks chromatically upwards to arrive at E at the beginning of bar 3. A similar idea is used in bar 3 to connect the E^7 and B^7 chords.

B Section (Bars 5–20)

This section starts with a stop-time section, within which the bass plays a simple riff at the end of each bar before stopping to leave room for the guitar fills.

Bars 5–20 | *Format*

Breaking from the 12-bar blues format, this song features a slightly extended format of 16 bars. The only difference is that it has eight bars of E^7 at the beginning instead of four.

Bars 5–11 | *Stabs*

The bass plays a staccato note at the beginning of each bar here, then a three-note figure at the end to lead into the next bar with the aim of leaving space for the guitar fills.

Bar 13–20 | *Blues groove*

An eighth-note groove is established from bar 13 onwards. This part is based on chord tones, with some chromatic passing notes to smooth the transition between chords. For example, bar 13 consists of chord tones from the A^7 chord: root (A), octave (A), 7th (G) and 5th (E). The following bar does not have the 5th, using instead the notes D and D♯ to ascend to the E^7 chord in the following bar.

Bars 12–20 | *Staccato notes*

Throughout this section you will notice how the first note of each pair of eighth notes is marked staccato (Fig. 2). Playing the first note staccato will help with the shuffle feel.

C Section (Bars 21–32)

The C section is an opportunity for you to improvise your own line. This section is a simple 12-bar blues format rather than the 16-bar format used earlier.

Bars 21–28 | *Improvising*

You can improvise your own line over these eight bars. You are free to play as you wish but you should create a part that is in keeping with the style of the piece. You may wish to incorporate some of the ideas already heard in the piece (but not the actual parts).

Bars 29–30 | *Accents*

The first two notes of each of these bars are accented, so play them a little louder. The second note of each bar is an octave higher and falls on the '&' of the second beat. As this is the shorter of the eighth notes (remember the swing feel), this note will be played just before the third beat of the bar. It is then tied to the third beat and ends with a slide downwards.

D Section (Bars 33–49)

This final section of the song follows the 16-bar blues format and has a continuous walking eighth-note bassline.

Bar 34 | *Triplet*

The triplet played on the fourth beat of this bar is reused in later bars in this section. Triplets are three notes played evenly on a beat and occur naturally in the swing feel. Be sure to play all three notes evenly.

Bar 48 | *Blues ending*

As the 16-bar sequence ends, a chord of F^7 is played just before the final E chord. This is a classic blues ending.

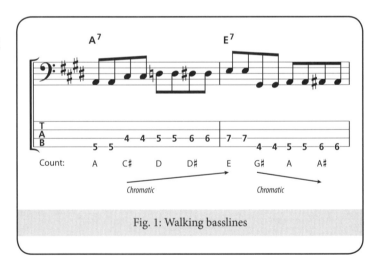

Fig. 1: Walking basslines

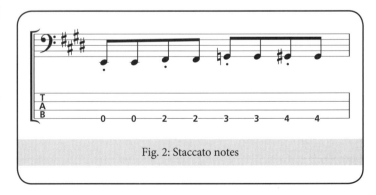

Fig. 2: Staccato notes

SONG TITLE: INDECISIVE

GENRE: POP PUNK

TEMPO: 155 BPM

KEY: C MAJOR

TECH FEATURES: TIGHT STACCATO GROOVES

USE OF SPACE

EIGHTH-NOTE

SYNCOPATIONS

COMPOSER: JAMES UINGS

PERSONNEL: STUART RYAN (GTR)

HENRY THOMAS (BASS)

NOAM LEDERMAN (DRUMS)

OVERVIEW

'Indecisive' is a pop punk song written in the style of bands such as Green Day, Blink-182 and The Offspring. The bassline for this song is predominantly a supportive part that is crafted around a solid, staccato, root-based groove. The use of space is important in this particular line, as is locking in tightly with the drummer.

STYLE FOCUS

Pop punk songs typically combine the fast tempos and attitude of classic punk music with the catchy melodies and vocal harmonies of pop. Pop punk bassists need the ability to play fast melodic basslines, pumping staccato grooves and lines that can often serve as one of the main melodic features of the song. Most pop punk bass guitarists favour using a pick. To enhance the band's pop punk look, feel and sound, they frequently wear their guitars slung low.

THE BIGGER PICTURE

The combination of pop and punk was first heard in the 1970s courtesy of bands like Buzzcocks, Ramones and The Undertones. The genre differs

from traditional punk in its lyrical content (far less political), its focus on melody and vocal harmonies, and its more polished musical and production values. Pop punk enjoyed a resurgence in the mid 1990s thanks largely to bands such as Green Day and The Offspring. By the end of the decade, Blink-182, Sum 41 and Less Than Jake joined Green Day and The Offspring to create a pop punk phenomenon that dominated the charts and music channels such as MTV and Kerrang! TV.

Pop punk bands often have the same instrumentation as classic punk: bass, drums, guitars and vocals. However, keys are often used, particularly in the studio, and harmony vocals are an important part of the sound. There are some exciting bass players working in the genre, including Blink-182's Mark Hoppus and Green Day's Mike Dirnt.

RECOMMENDED LISTENING

There is a wealth of pop punk albums, but *Dookie* (1994), *Warning* (2000) and *American Idiot* (2004) by Green Day, and the songs 'Basket Case', 'Warning', 'Minority' and 'American Idiot' are stand-outs. *Enema Of The State* (1999) by Blink-182 also sports an exciting collection of basslines, particularly on 'What's My Age Again?' and 'All The Small Things'.

Indecisive

James Uings

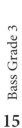

Walkthrough

A Section (Bars 1–8)
The opening section establishes the feel of the song; a pounding, eighth-note rhythm played at a fast tempo.

Bars 1–3 | *Eighth notes*
The majority of the first section is played as eighth notes. These should be played evenly in volume and tone.

Bar 4 | *More eighth notes*
This bar features two eighth-notes on the third beat. One beat can be split evenly into two eighth notes, so ensure they are the same length when you play them. You can get a feel for the eighth-note pulse by counting "1 & 2 & 3 & 4 &".

B Section (Bars 9–16)
The B section consists of the bass playing stabs and a motif that is used throughout the piece.

Bar 12 | *Ties*
This bar consists of a group of six eighth notes starting on beat one (Fig. 1). The final eighth note, on the '&' of beat three, is tied into beat four. This means you should let the last eighth note ring for the remainder of the bar.

C Section (Bars 17–24)
This section starts off with the eighth-note rhythm used earlier before changing to a busier eighth-note pattern.

Bars 21–25 | *Eighth-note rests*
The rhythm used in these bars is an eighth-note rhythm but with rests on the second and fourth beats (Fig. 2), and a note played on the '&' of these beats. Count "1 & 2 & 3 & 4 &", playing a note on every count except '2' and '4'.

D Section (Bars 25–32)
This section is similar to the B section but with extra bass notes added for harmonic interest.

Bar 25 | *Extra chord tones*
There are two eighth notes (E and C) on beat four instead of a rest. The C is the root note of the chord. The E is also a chord tone: the major third is used to reinforce the harmony.

E Section (Bars 33–46)
This section with the guitar solo enables you to develop your own bass part. The second part of the section is comprised of eighth-note rhythms similar to those used earlier.

Bars 33–40 | *Developing a part*
Here you can develop your own part. Try to craft one in

keeping with the track but with added melody. Basing your line on the root, third and fifth of the chords would be a great place to start.

F Section (Bars 47–54)
The F section is a bass solo where you can improvise a melodic bass part.

Bars 47–50 | *Bass solo*
The bass is the melodic instrument for these four bars. Try to base your improvisational ideas on simple chord tones and do not over-complicate your solo.

G Section (Bars 55–66)
The final section brings together many of the ideas used previously but develops them rhythmically and melodically.

Bars 59–61 | *Root and fifth*
The bass alternates between the root and fifth of the chord. The fifth is on the same fret but played on the string below.

Bars 62–64 | *Octave lines*
These feature the same unison fill, except they are played in different octaves. When playing this line, aim for a consistent volume in each bar: try not to let the notes on the low E string sound louder than those on the D string.

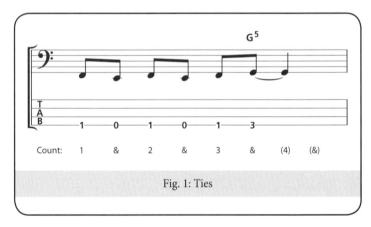

Fig. 1: Ties

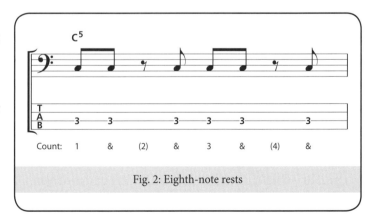

Fig. 2: Eighth-note rests

SONG TITLE: MAIDEN VOYAGE

GENRE: INDIE ROCK

TEMPO: 130 BPM

KEY: E MAJOR

TECH FEATURES: TIED NOTES

BASS SOLO

PART DEVELOPMENT

COMPOSER: JOE BENNETT

PERSONNEL: STUART RYAN (GTR)

HENRY THOMAS (BASS)

JOE BENNETT (KEYS)

NOAM LEDERMAN (DRUMS)

OVERVIEW

'Maiden Voyage' is an indie rock track in the style of bands like The Killers, Arcade Fire and Coldplay. Indie rock offers a wealth of opportunities for melodic bass playing; therefore, the bassist's role within the genre is an interesting one. This track offers a mix of solid supportive lines and melodic passages, tied notes and a bass solo.

STYLE FOCUS

Unlike its 'classic' and 'hard' counterparts, indie rock is not usually based on unison riffs played by the guitar and bass. The instrumentation is also more varied, and keyboards and synths are common. Because he is not tied to riffing with the guitar, the bassist has the opportunity to play more creative parts. Fingerstyle and pick playing are both appropriate, and 'Maiden Voyage' can be played with either technique.

THE BIGGER PICTURE

Indie rock melds many sub-genres of rock with elements of pop music and even disco, new wave and punk. While indie is still predominantly guitar driven,

many contemporary groups are also influenced by synth pop, a genre that was popularised in the 1980s by groups such as Duran Duran, Spandau Ballet and Pet Shop Boys. This influence is evident in their use of vintage synthesizers and dance style drum beats. The Killers and Coldplay have both been known to incorporate musical elements running from laptops in their live performances.

There are several bassists from the 1980s who remain influential, including John Taylor (Duran Duran) and Peter Hook (New Order). Mark Stoermer (The Killers), Guy Berryman (Coldplay) and Chris Wolstenholme (Muse) fly the flag for contemporary indie rock bass.

RECOMMENDED LISTENING

You will notice an obvious synth pop influence on The Killers' debut *Hot Fuss* (2004), which includes the singles 'Jenny Was A Friend Of Mine', 'Mr. Brightside' and 'Somebody Told Me'. Arcade Fire are a critically acclaimed seven-piece band from Montreal, Canada. Their first three records (*Funeral*, *Neon Bible* and *The Suburbs*) are concept albums with a more serious, less pop direction than many of their contemporaries. Coldplay's sound has evolved to include electronics, as on 2011's *Mylo Xyloto*.

Maiden Voyage

Joe Bennett

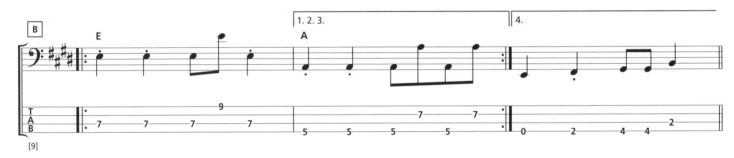

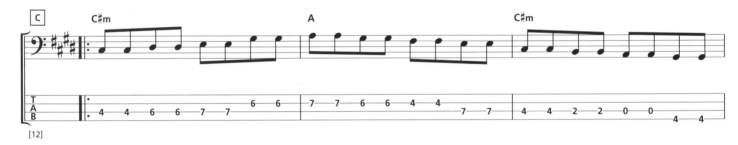

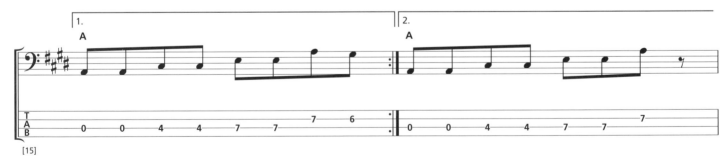

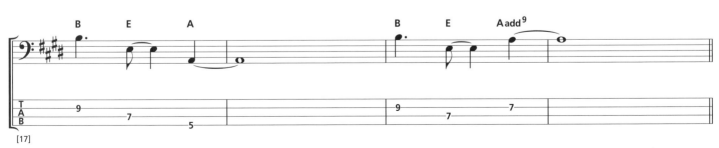

Walkthrough

A Section (Bars 1–8)
The intro to this song features the synth prominently and has a bassline that makes use of ties and syncopations.

Bars 1–8 | *Syncopated rhythms*
Syncopated rhythms are used in the first bar. The first note is a half note tied to the first eighth note of the third beat. The second note, a quarter note, falls on the '&' of beat three, with the final note in the bar falling on the '&' of beat four.

Bars 5–8 | *Lower octaves*
In the second half of the intro, the same line is played but with many of the notes an octave lower. This adds variety to the part. One possible fingering would be your fourth finger on the E, then a position shift to put your third on the G♯. This will enable you to play the A with your fourth finger, the G♯ with your third, and the F♯ with your first.

B Section (Bars 9–11)
This section is based on a quarter-note foundation.

Bars 9–11 | *Staccato quarter notes*
Throughout this section, the bass plays staccato notes (Fig. 1). These need to be played accurately, so listen to the drums and aim to lock in as tightly as you can.

Bars 9–10 | *Playing octaves*
When playing the octave patterns in these bars, use the first finger of your fretting hand for the first note and your fourth finger to play the octave. Ensure that you are muting the other strings with the remaining fingers of your fretting hand. For example, when playing the octaves in bar 9, your second finger can rest against the E string to prevent it from ringing out.

C Section (Bars 12–20)
The bass takes things up a gear in the C section with a melodic, continuous eighth-note line. The second half of this section is a syncopated chord section in which the bass outlines the progression using root notes.

Bars 12–16 | *Fingerings*
The eighth-note bassline used for this section is a great example of a bass melody. Fret the C♯ with your first finger to enable you to play the remainder of the notes in this two-bar section using the one-finger-per-fret system.

D Section (Bars 21–28)
This section of the song features a melodic bass solo that is eight bars long. The first four bars are written; the second four bars are your opportunity to develop the line.

Bars 21–28 | *Learning the bass solo*
As you learn this solo, think of it as a melody line. Listen to it several times before putting your hands on your instrument and learning the notes.

E Section (Bars 29–36)
This part of the song features a melodic bass figure that is repeated in each bar. Note, however, that it follows a different root note each time.

Bars 29–36 | *Repeated melodic figure*
In this section, a repeated figure is used. After the initial dotted quarter note in each bar, a three-note phrase is played from the E at the 9th fret of the G string. This phrase remains the same, although the root note at the beginning of the bar changes to follow the chords. A suggested fingering is shown below (Fig. 2).

F Section (Bars 37–46)
This part has a straight eighth-note bassline, with scope for you to embellish it the second time around.

Bars 37–40 | *Developing a part*
This second time through you can develop the bassline. Try adding a little more movement but do not overcomplicate the part. Your job here is to support the guitar solo.

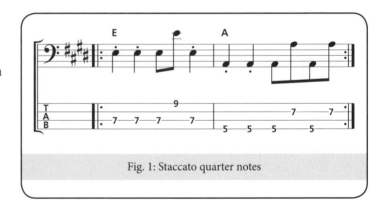

Fig. 1: Staccato quarter notes

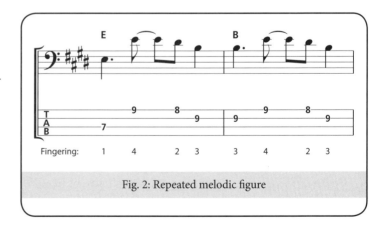

Fig. 2: Repeated melodic figure

SONG TITLE: RASTA MONKEY

GENRE: REGGAE

TEMPO: 156 BPM

KEY: G MINOR

TECH FEATURES: MELODIC BASSLINES
TRIPLET GROOVE
STACCATO NOTES

COMPOSER: NOAM LEDERMAN

PERSONNEL: STUART RYAN (GTR)
HENRY THOMAS (BASS)
NOAM LEDERMAN (DRUMS)
ROSS STANLEY (KEYS)
FERGUS GERRAND (PERC)

OVERVIEW

'Rasta Monkey' is a reggae track written in the style of popular reggae artists such as Bob Marley, Peter Tosh and Black Uhuru. The bassline for this song is a classic reggae line that sets up an initial groove that is embellished throughout the song. Reggae is all about feel, so locking in with the drums is crucial.

STYLE FOCUS

The bass is one of the most important instruments in a reggae group. With the guitar simply playing 'skank' rhythms, the bass player needs to underpin the song with an unobtrusive but catchy melodic bassline. While improvisation is important when playing reggae, the bassist should not play extravagantly.

THE BIGGER PICTURE

Reggae is the music of Jamaica, and gained worldwide success and appeal through the hits of Bob Marley, who remains reggae's undisputed superstar. The genre developed in Jamaica in the late 1960s, as a progression of its more uptempo predecessors ska and rocksteady. In fact, Jamaican music became progressively slower through this development from ska to rocksteady to reggae. The key feature of the style is its accent on the offbeat, known as the 'skank'.

Marley and his band The Wailers are the best known exponents of the style; other pioneers include Jimmy Cliff and Toots And The Maytals. The genre is said to have got its name from the latter's 1968 single 'Do The Reggay' (the 'y' replaced with the familiar 'e'). The rock and pop audiences of the British and American mainstream weren't drawn to the genre until Eric Clapton had a top 10 hit with his cover of Marley's 'I Shot The Sheriff' in 1974.

Reggae relies heavily on the bass and the instrument's status has made stars of many players: Aston Barrett (Bob Marley), Robbie Shakespeare (Black Uhuru) and Errol 'Flabba' Holt (Roots Radics).

RECOMMENDED LISTENING

Listen to Bob Marley's *Legend* (1984), featuring his biggest hits 'Is This Love', 'No Woman No Cry', 'Could You Be Loved', 'I Shot the Sheriff' and 'Jamming'. *Legalize It* (1976) by Peter Tosh is also recommended. *Essential Skatalites* (2011) by the Skatalites is classic ska, while The Specials' self-titled debut album (1979) represents the British ska revival movement, often referred to as 2 Tone.

Rasta Monkey

Noam Lederman

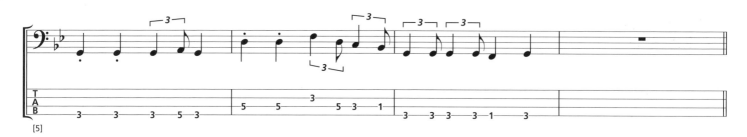

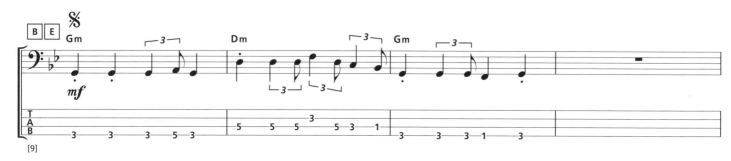

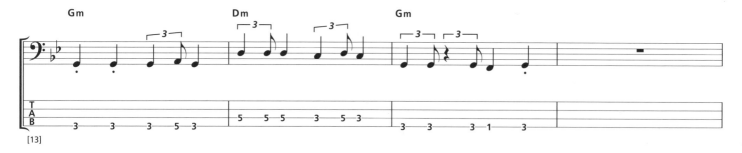

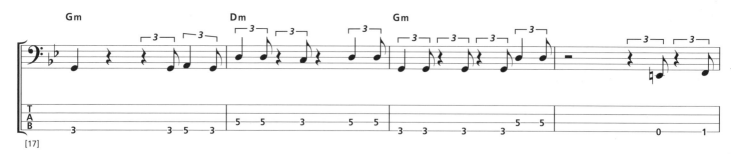

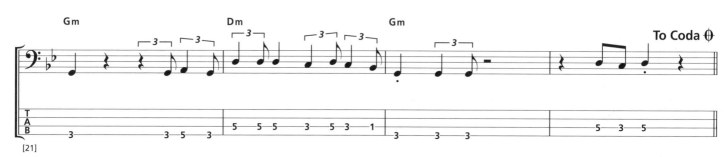

Bass Grade 3

22

Walkthrough

A Section (Bars 1–8)
This section of the track establishes the reggae groove and swing triplet feel used in the first part of the song.

Bars 1–8 | *Triplet groove*
As you can see, throughout this section there is a quarter note followed by an eighth-note rhythm, with a triplet bracket over the top. The result of this is a longer note followed by a shorter note. Before you begin tackling this line, listen carefully to the CD in order to become accustomed to the feel of the track.

Bars 1–8 | *Staccato dots*
Many of the quarter notes are marked with staccato dots during this section (Fig. 1). It is important to adhere to these very closely, because they will enable you to capture the feel of the track.

B Section (Bars 9–24)
The B section is a variation of the A section that supports the guitar melody. From bar 17 the part develops and uses more space. This is an important element of reggae grooves.

Bar 17 | *Rhythmic accuracy*
After playing the first note of this bar on beat one, the bass rests before re-entering on the upbeat of beat three. Because this is notated using triplets, the upbeat is the shorter of the two notes in the beat (the first note being a quarter-note rest), so the final three notes in this bar should be played short-long-short. The swing feel will be very obvious in this three note phrase and you will be able to hear how it sets up the next bar perfectly.

C Section (Bars 25–40)
This section features a change of feel, in that the swing flavour has been replaced by a straight eighth-note feel.

Bar 25 | *Change of feel*
In this section of the song, the feel changes to a straight feel. This is indicated by the fact that the eighth notes are marked as straight eighth notes rather than triplet rhythms.

Bar 28 | *Bass fill*
This bar features a simple yet effective bass fill (Fig. 2). The recommended fingering is to use one-finger-per-fret. Play the G on the E string with your first finger of the fretting hand then play the B♭ with your fourth. The remaining notes can then be played with your first, second and third fingers.

Bar 36 | *Bass fill*
One possible fingering for this fill would be to fret the G and F notes on the D string with your fourth and first fingers

respectively. You can then use your fourth to fret the D on the A string below. After this, you should move your hand so that the C is played with your fourth finger, leaving your hand in position to play the B♭ with your first finger. This position shift also means that you can play the next part of the line without shifting position again.

D & E Sections (Bars 41–51)
This D section features the guitar solo and provides you with the opportunity to create your own accompanying bass guitar part beneath it.

The E section is simply a reprise of the B section and leads into the Coda.

Bars 41–51 | *Developing a part*
When playing your own part beneath the guitar solo, begin by basing your line on bass parts that have already been used throughout the song and parts that fit with the chord progression. As you become comfortable with the line you can begin to develop it and put your own stamp on it, but remember to keep the groove solid.

Bar 48 | *Navigation*
At the end of this bar you are directed back to the sign at letter B. This part of the song is played with the triplet groove. At the end of bar 23 you are directed to the Coda, which is played with a straight feel.

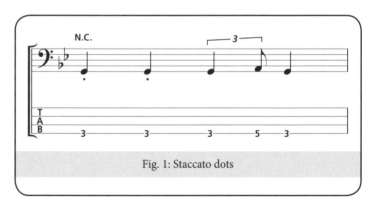

Fig. 1: Staccato dots

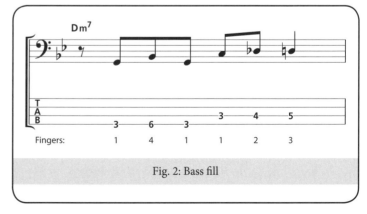

Fig. 2: Bass fill

SONG TITLE: FALLOUT

GENRE: METAL

TEMPO: 75 BPM

KEY: E MINOR

TECH FEATURES: UNISON RIFFING
SYNCOPATION
DOUBLE TIME FEEL

COMPOSER: CHARLIE GRIFFITHS
& JASON BOWLD

PERSONNEL: CHARLIE GRIFFITHS (GTR)
DAVE MARKS (BASS)
NOAM LEDERMAN (DRUMS)

OVERVIEW

'Fallout' is a track written in the style of proto metal bands Led Zeppelin and Deep Purple, and the first actual metal band, Black Sabbath. You will find its bassline a challenge because it doubles most of the guitar riffs and anchors the band through some tricky syncopations and double time feel sections.

STYLE FOCUS

Many bassists find heavy metal an exciting style to play. While the bass often anchors the band with eighth-note-based root note grooves, it frequently doubles the menacing sounding guitar riffs too. There is plenty of scope for improvisation within this style, usually under the guitar solo.

THE BIGGER PICTURE

Generally speaking, the musicians in Black Sabbath, Deep Purple and Led Zeppelin came from a blues rock background, but during the 1960s and 1970s they began exploring new boundaries, adding brute force to their playing and, in the case of the guitarists, pushing their amps to new limits of distortion. In doing so, they laid the foundations of heavy metal. The 1980s built on these foundations and welcomed a New Wave of British Heavy Metal (NWBHM) with bands including Iron Maiden, Judas Priest and Diamond Head gaining worldwide attention and, in turn, inspiring Metallica (among others) who spearheaded the thrash scene.

Many iconic bass players can be found in the early days of heavy metal: Steve Harris (Iron Maiden), Geezer Butler (Black Sabbath), Lemmy (Motörhead) and John Paul Jones (Led Zeppelin) are all legendary players from this era who are as influential today as they were then.

RECOMMENDED LISTENING

Recommended heavy metal albums include *Paranoid* by Black Sabbath, featuring the classic songs 'War Pigs', 'Iron Man' and the hit title track. Early Iron Maiden albums are also interesting, particularly *The Number Of The Beast* (1982) featuring 'Run To The Hills' with its classic Maiden 'gallop' rhythm and their *Powerslave* (1984), which boasts fan favourites 'Aces High', '2 Minutes To Midnight' and the album's namesake. Although it is not strictly speaking a metal album, Motörhead's *The Ace Of Spades* (1980) is interesting for its aggressive, almost thrash-like grooves which influenced metal bands of the 1980s.

Fallout

Charlie Griffiths and Jason Bowld

Walkthrough

A Section (Bars 1–4)
This section opens with a powerful riff featuring syncopated parts. These rhythms may look challenging, but are actually quite easy to pick up by ear and are explained fully below.

Bar 1 | *Sixteenth-note rhythms*
This bar features several 16th note and eighth note combinations. The first, on beat one, is two 16th notes followed by an eighth note. When you play this, ensure that the first two notes are played in quick succession and that the third note (E) falls on the upbeat.

Bar 2 | *Syncopation*
The first four notes of this bar are heavily syncopated. The first (E) is played on beat one, with the second (B) falling on the final 16th note of the beat. You may find it easier to think of this note as falling just before beat two. The third note (D) falls on the upbeat of beat two, and the final note (A) falls on the second 16th note of the third beat. It might help you to learn this by thinking of this note as falling just after the downbeat of beat three.

B Section (Bars 5–8)
The aggressive unison riff used in this section sounds even more menacing because of the slow tempo.

Bar 5 | *Fingering*
Because this riff is played entirely on the E string, you will need to consider the fingering you use carefully (Fig. 1). One possible fingering would be to play the opening B and B♭ with your third and fourth fingers then shift down one fret so you can play the B♭ and A with your third and fourth fingers after the open string. This will enable you to play the G at the end of the second beat with your first finger. Work slowly and only increase speed when you are comfortable.

C Section (Bars 9–12)
This section is almost identical to the A section, except with some variations on the parts that are already established.

D Section (Bars 13–17)
The D section is a variation of the B section that uses syncopation and wide interval leaps.

Bars 13–14 | *Syncopation*
The first half of bar 13 is played in the same manner as described in the notes for the B section. However, on the third and fourth beats you will find two syncopated notes. The first, an A, falls on the upbeat of beat three. The second syncopated note, a B♭, is played on the second 16th note of the fourth beat.

E Section (Bars 18–21)
This section features the riff from the B section transposed to A, with added notes that are bent upwards.

Bar 18 | *Quarter-tone bends*
All of the C notes in this bar are marked with quarter-tone bends (Fig. 2). This does not need to be exact, so all you are required to do is bend each note slightly. To do this, simply pull downwards on the string a little with the finger that is fretting the note.

Bar 19 | *The blues scale*
The A blues scale (a common scale in heavy metal) is used in this bar for the descending run on beats three and four. If you start this fill with the first finger of your fretting hand on the first note (C), you will notice how this part falls neatly under the fingers.

F Section (Bars 22–26)
The final section of the song is a repeat of the first section, with some added rhythmic embellishments.

Bar 25 | *Triplets*
The song ends with a group of triplets on the third and fourth beats of this bar. When playing these triplets, be sure to play them evenly (i.e. three notes in the space of one). You can vocalise this by repeating a three syllable word like 'ev-en-ly' to get used to how triplets should sound.

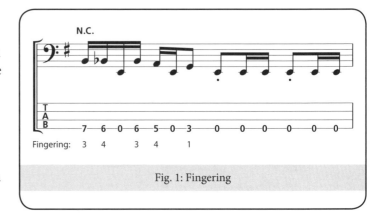
Fig. 1: Fingering

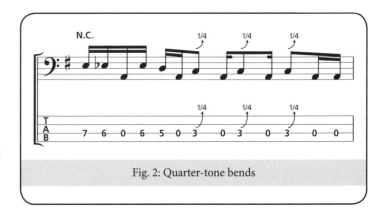
Fig. 2: Quarter-tone bends

Technical Exercises

In this section the examiner will ask you to play a selection of exercises drawn from each of the three groups shown below. Groups A and B contain examples of the scales and arpeggios you can use when playing the pieces. In Group C you will be asked to prepare the bassline riff exercise and play it to the backing track in the exam. You do not need to memorise the exercises (and can use the book in the exam) but the examiner will be looking for the speed of your response. The examiner will also give credit for the level of your musicality.

Groups A and B should be prepared on the starting notes of G, A and B. Before you start the section you will be asked whether you would like to play the exercises along with the click or hear a single bar of click before you commence the test. The tempo is ♩ = 90.

Group A: Scales
1. Major scale (G major scale shown)

2. Natural minor scale (B natural minor scale shown)

3. Minor pentatonic scale (B minor pentatonic scale shown)

4. Major pentatonic scale (G major pentatonic scale shown)

5. Blues scale (A blues scale shown)

Group B: Arpeggios
One octave and should be played both ascending and descending

1. Major arpeggio (A major arpeggio shown)

2. Minor arpeggio (B minor arpeggio shown)

3. Dominant ^{7} arpeggio (G dominant ^{7} arpeggio shown)

Group C: Bassline Riff

In the exam you will be asked to play the following riff to a backing track. The riff shown in bars 1 and 2 should be played in the same shape in bars 3–8. The root note of the pattern to be played is shown in the music in bars 3, 5 and 7. The tempo is ♩=90.

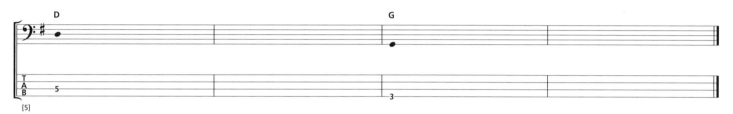

Sight Reading

In this section you have a choice between either a sight reading test or an improvisation and interpretation test (see facing page). You will be asked to prepare a sight reading test which will be given to you by the examiner. The test is a four bar melody in the key of G major or A minor. The examiner will allow you 90 seconds to prepare it and will set the tempo for you. The tempo is ♩ = 80.

Improvisation & Interpretation

You will be asked to play an improvised bassline to a backing track of four bars in the keys of either G major or A minor. You have 30 seconds to prepare then you will be allowed to practise during the first playing of the backing track before playing it to the examiner on the second playing of the backing track. This test is continuous with a one bar count-in at the beginning and after the practice session. The tempo is ♩ = 80–90.

Ear Tests

There are two ear tests in this grade. The examiner will play each test to you twice. You will find one example of each type of test printed below.

Test 1: Melodic Recall

The examiner will play you a two bar melody with a drum backing using the G minor pentatonic scale. The first note of the melody will be the root note and the first interval will be ascending. You will play the melody back on your instrument. You will hear the test twice.

Each time the test is played it is preceded by a one bar count-in. There will be a short gap for you to practise after you have heard the test for the second time. Next you will hear a vocal count-in and you will then play the melody to the drum backing. The tempo is ♩=85.

Test 2: Rhythmic Recall

The examiner will play you a two bar rhythm played to a drum backing on the E string. You will hear the test twice. You will be asked to play the rhythm back. You will then be asked to identify the rhythm from two printed examples shown to you.

Each time the test is played it is preceded by a one bar count-in. There will be a short gap for you to practise. Next you will hear a vocal count-in and you will then play the rhythm to the drum backing. The tempo is ♩=90.

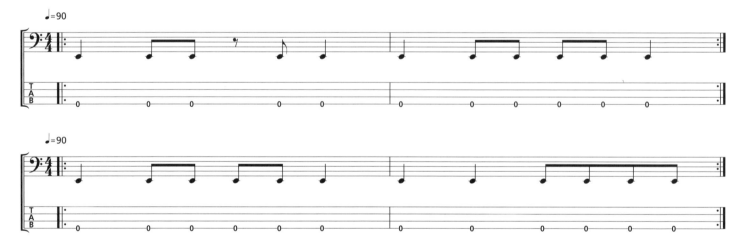

General Musicianship Questions

In this part of the exam you will be asked five questions. Four of these questions will be about general music knowledge and the fifth question will be asked about your instrument.

Music Knowledge

The examiner will ask you four music knowledge questions based on a piece of music that you have played in the exam. You will nominate the piece of music about which the questions will be asked.

In Grade 3, you will be asked:

- Names of pitches

- The meaning of the time signature marking

- Whole, half, quarter, eighth note, triplet eighth note and 16th note values

- Rest values

- The construction of a major or a minor chord

Instrument Knowledge

The examiner will also ask you one question regarding your instrument.

In Grade 3 you will be asked to identify:

- The following parts of your bass – neck, fretboard, body, tuning-pegs, nut, pick-ups, scratch plate, jack socket and bridge

- The location of the volume and tone controls on your bass

- The location of the volume/gain controls on the amp

Further Information

Tips on how to approach this part of this exam can be found in the *Syllabus Guide* for bass, the Rockschool *Bass Companion Guide* and on the Rockschool website: *www.rockschool.co.uk.*

Entering Rockschool Exams

Entering a Rockschool exam is easy. You may enter either online at *www.rockschool.co.uk* or by downloading and filling in an exam entry form. Information on current exam fees can be obtained from Rockschool online or by calling +44 (0)845 460 4747.

- You should enter for your exam when you feel ready.

- You may enter for any one of the three examination periods shown below with their closing dates:

EXAMINATION PERIODS

PERIOD	DURATION	CLOSING DATE
Period A	1st February to 31st March	1st December
Period B	1st May to 31st July	1st April
Period C	23rd October to 15th December	1st October

These dates apply from 1st September 2012 until further notice

- The full Rockschool examination terms and conditions can be downloaded from our website. The information shown below is a summary.

- Please complete your entry with the information required. Fill in the type and level of exam and instrument, along with the examination period and year. Paper entry forms should be sent with a cheque or postal order (payable to Rockschool Ltd) to the address shown on the entry form. Entry forms sent by post will be acknowledged either by letter or email, while all entries made online will automatically be acknowledged by email.

- Applications received after the expiry of the closing date, whether made by post or online, may be accepted subject to the payment of a late fee.

- Rockschool will allocate your exam to a specific centre and you will receive notification of the exam showing a date, location and time, as well as advice on what to bring to the centre. We endeavour to give you four weeks notice ahead of your exam date.

- You should inform Rockschool of any cancellations or alterations to the schedule as soon as you can because it may not be possible to transfer entries from one centre, or one period, to another without the payment of an additional fee.

- Please bring your music book and CD to the exam. You may use photocopied music if this helps you avoid awkward page turns. The examiner will sign each book during each examination. Please note, you may be barred from taking an exam if you use someone else's music.

- You should aim to arrive for your exam 15 minutes before the time stated on the schedule. Guitarists and bass players should get ready to enter the exam room by taking their instrument from its case and tuning up. This will help with the smooth running of each exam day.

- Each Grade 3 exam is scheduled to last 25 minutes. You can use a small proportion of this time to set up and check the sound levels.

- You will receive a copy of the examiner's marksheet two to three weeks after the exam. If you have passed you will also receive a Rockschool certificate of achievement.

Bass Grade 3 Marking Schemes

ELEMENT	PASS	MERIT	DISTINCTION
Performance Piece 1	12–14 out of 20	15–17 out of 20	18+ out of 20
Performance Piece 2	12–14 out of 20	15–17 out of 20	18+ out of 20
Performance Piece 3	12–14 out of 20	15–17 out of 20	18+ out of 20
Technical Exercises	9–10 out of 15	11–12 out of 15	13+ out of 15
Either **Sight Reading** *or* **Improvisation & Interpretation**	6 out of 10	7–8 out of 10	9+ out of 10
Ear Tests	6 out of 10	7–8 out of 10	9+ out of 10
General Musicianship Questions	3 out of 5	4 out of 5	5 out of 5
TOTAL MARKS	**60%+**	**74%+**	**90%+**

Performance Certificates | Grades 1–8

ELEMENT	PASS	MERIT	DISTINCTION
Performance Piece 1	12–14 out of 20	15–17 out of 20	18+ out of 20
Performance Piece 2	12–14 out of 20	15–17 out of 20	18+ out of 20
Performance Piece 3	12–14 out of 20	15–17 out of 20	18+ out of 20
Performance Piece 4	12–14 out of 20	15–17 out of 20	18+ out of 20
Performance Piece 5	12–14 out of 20	15–17 out of 20	18+ out of 20
TOTAL MARKS	**60%+**	**75%+**	**90%+**

Bass Guitar Notation Explained

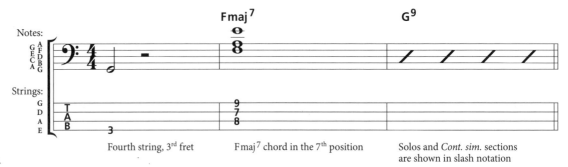

THE MUSICAL STAVE shows pitches and rhythms and is divided by lines into bars. Pitches are named after the first seven letters of the alphabet.

TABLATURE graphically represents the bass guitar fingerboard. Each horizontal line represents a string and each number represents a fret.

Fourth string, 3rd fret

Fmaj7 chord in the 7th position

Solos and *Cont. sim.* sections are shown in slash notation

Definitions For Special Bass Guitar Notation

HAMMER-ON: Pick the lower note then sound the higher note by fretting it without picking.

PULL-OFF: Pick the higher note then sound the lower note by lifting your finger without picking.

SLIDE: Pick the first note and slide to the next. If the line connects (as below) the second note is *not* repicked.

GLISSANDO: Slide off of a note at the end of its rhythmic value. The note that follows *is* repicked.

SLAP STYLE: Slap bass technique is indicated through the letters T (thumb) and P (pull).

TAPPING: Sound note by tapping the string – circles denote a picking hand tap, squares a fretting hand tap.

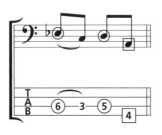

DEAD (GHOST) NOTES: Pick the string while the note is muted by your fretting hand.

NATURAL HARMONICS: Lightly touch the string above the indicated fret then pick to sound a harmonic.

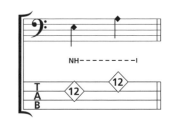

 (accent) — Accentuate note (play it louder).

 (staccato) — Shorten time value of note.

 — Fermata (Pause)

D.%. al Coda — Go back to the sign (%), then play until the bar marked **To Coda** ⊕ then skip to the section marked ⊕ **Coda**.

D.C. al Fine — Go back to the beginning of the song and play until the bar marked **Fine** (end).

 — Repeat the bars between the repeat signs.

 — When a repeated section has different endings, play the first ending only the first time and the second ending only the second time.

SONG TITLE: 223

GENRE: POP PUNK

TEMPO: 165 BPM

KEY: D MAJOR

TECH FEATURES: RIFFING ON ONE STRING

FAST TEMPOS

DYNAMICS

COMPOSER: JAMES UINGS

PERSONNEL: STUART RYAN (GTR)

DAVE MARKS (BASS)

NOAM LEDERMAN (DRUMS)

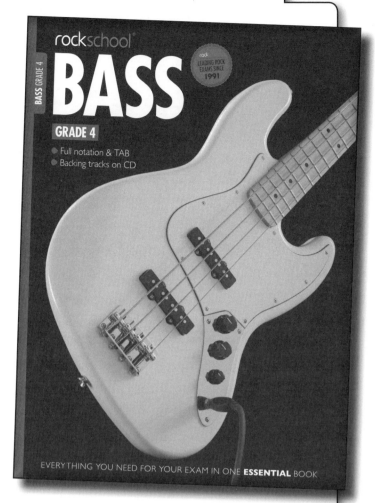

OVERVIEW

'223' is a fast-paced pop punk track written in the style of bands such as Blink-182, The Offspring, Sum 41 and Green Day. Pop punk basslines are often melodic, riff-based and tough to play due to the fast tempos used within the genre. This piece can be played either with the fingers or a pick, although for a true pop punk tone a pick is recommended.

STYLE FOCUS

Pop punk is a combination of the fast tempos and chord progressions of punk fused with the catchy melodies of pop. The pop punk bassist will need the ability to play fast, melodic basslines that support the song and drive it forward. These basslines can often be memorable, and it is not uncommon for them to serve as counter melodies.

THE BIGGER PICTURE

This blend of pop and punk styles has proved extremely durable over the last three decades. Early pop punk bands included Buzzcocks, Ramones and The Undertones, who were all discernible from their punk peers thanks to their strong melodies and less political lyrical content. Pop punk became popular again during the mid-1990s thanks to bands such

as Green Day and The Offspring, the latter of which found mainstream success through tracks like 'Come Out And Play'.

By the end of the 1990s pop punk had become a worldwide phenomenon and Blink-182, Less Than Jake and Sum 41, among others, enjoyed widespread popularity alongside existing pop punk groups like the aforementioned Green Day and The Offspring.

The focal point of pop punk is often the guitars or the vocals, but bassists Mike Dirnt (Green Day), Greg K (The Offspring) and Mark Hoppus (Blink-182) attract more attention than bassists in some other genres, thanks to the melodic flavour of pop punk.

RECOMMENDED LISTENING

Classic pop punk albums include Green Day's *Dookie* (1994), boasting their first big hit 'Longview', and *Warning* (2000), which includes the title track and 'Minority'. *Americana* by The Offspring (1998) is also recommended for Greg K's basslines on 'Pretty Fly (For a White Guy)'. *Enema of The State* (1999) by Blink-182 also offers a feel for pop punk basslines on 'What's My Age Again' and 'All The Small Things'.

223 (Grade 4 Preview)

James Uings

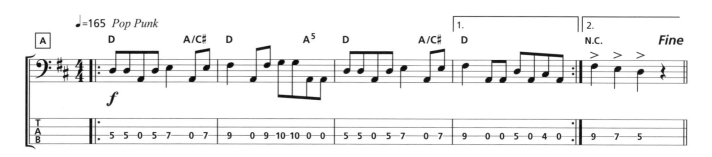

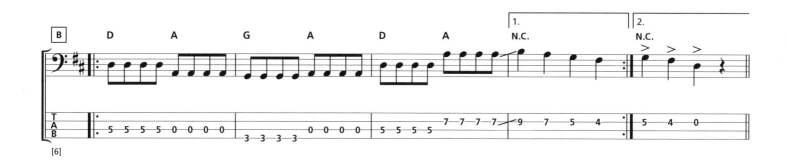

[6]

[11]

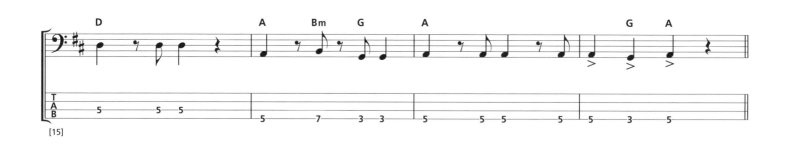

[15]

[19]

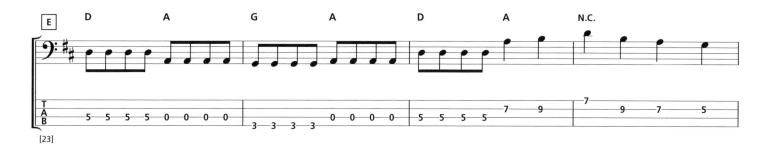

[23]

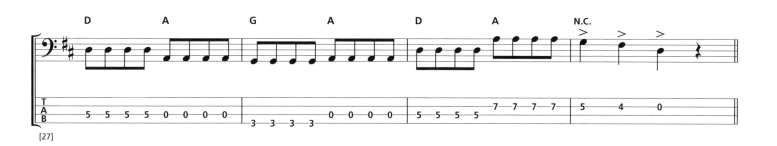

[27]

[31]

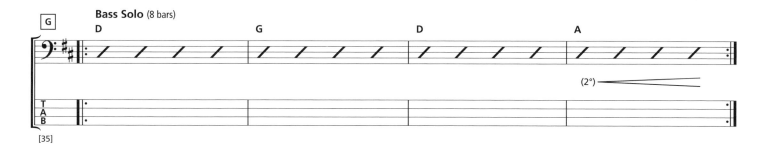

[35]

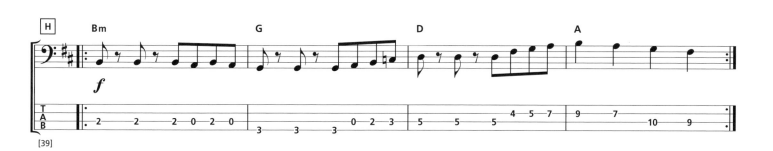

[39]

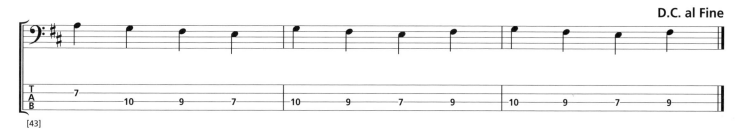

[43]

Bass Grade 3

Walkthrough (Grade 4 Preview)

A Section (Bars 1–6)
The intro to '223' has a melodic bassline that outlines the chord progression and is played entirely on one string.

Bars 1–6 | *Bass riff*
The bass riff that opens '223' is a melodic line based on chord tones, alternating with the open A string. Fret the D with your first finger then move up to fret the E at the end of the first bar with the same finger. Use your first and second fingers to play the F♯ and G notes.

Bars 1–6 | *Timing*
The bass is the featured instrument and for the first four bars the drums and guitar play minimal parts only. Focus on your timing because it will be noticeable if you slow down or speed up in between the drum and guitar hits.

B Section (Bars 6–10)
The B section is based on an eighth-note line that focuses on the root notes of the guitar chords.

Bars 6–8 | *Consistent eighth notes*
This is a continuous eighth-note line that must be played with a consistent attack throughout. If you are using a pick, play this part using up and downstrokes and ensure you produce the same level of attack and volume with each.

C Section (Bars 11–18)
A different feel is used for the verse. This is a classic pop punk progression and features some quick positional shifts.

Bar 14 | *Syncopation*
In this bar, there are some notes played on offbeats (Fig. 1). These occur on the offbeats of beats two and three. It can be tricky to count this rhythm at the song's fast tempo, so play this part slowly to begin with. Notes should fall on beat one, on the offbeats of beats two and three, then on beat four. Concentrate on locking in with the guitar.

D Section (Bars 19–22)
The bassline here has the same rhythmic pattern in the first three bars and locks in tightly with the drum part.

Bars 19–22 | *Rhythm*
The rhythm in this section is simpler than it looks. The first two notes are both eighth notes that fall on the first and second beats. These are followed by a group of four eighth notes played on the third and fourth beats.

Bars 19–22 | *Melodic lines*
Each chord is connected in the bassline by the group of four

eighth notes in each bar (Fig. 2). These groups are melodic lines that use diatonic notes to link the chords together.

E and F Sections (Bars 23–34)
The E section is essentially a repeat of the line from the B section. The F section has a light reggae feel with a simple yet effective bass part.

G Section (Bars 35–38)
The bass solo section is an opportunity to improvise a solo that fits the style of the song.

Bars 35–38 | *Soloing*
When planning your bass solo, consider the notes in each chord. Write these down then try to find melodic phrases that use these notes. You could take inspiration from the melodic linking phrases that were used in the bridge section.

H Section (Bars 39–45)
This is a repeat of the D section with some variations. There are also some navigation markings to be aware of.

Bar 45 | *Navigation*
At the end of the extended bridge section you are directed back to the beginning of the song, where the intro is played again as an outro. Be sure to stop at the direction 'Fine' at the end of the second time bar.

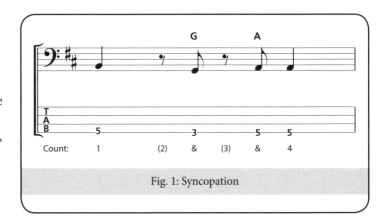

Fig. 1: Syncopation

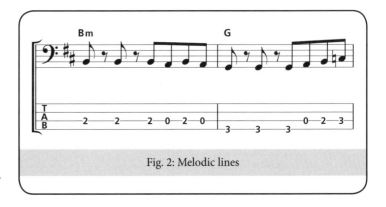

Fig. 2: Melodic lines